MERCURY FLATS
PUBLISHING
AN IMPRINT OF
ATOMIC MOUNTAIN PRESS, LLC

AF508282

BOOKS BY BEN DOUGLASS
PUBLISHED BY
MERCURY FLATS PUBLISHING

Beneath The Surface (Paperback)

The Last Cuppa: A One-Act Play
(Paperback)

Against The Grain: Poems of Liberation
(Paperback)

A Short Story Collection (Paperback)

The Restless Spirit: A Spiritual Memoir
(Paperback)

PERSONAL ESSAYS AND OTHER SUCH STUFF

BEN DOUGLASS
Author

RENE WALSH
Editor

MERCURY FLATS PUBLISHING

FIRST EDITION
Mercury Flats Publishing, ABN/DBA
Copyright © 2026 by Ronald Dwayne Douglass
ALL RIGHTS RESERVED

Library of Congress Control Number: 2026911027
ISBN: 979-8-9956219-1-1

Mercury Flats Publishing, ABN/DBA
[*an imprint of Atomic Mountain Press, L LC*]
5325 Northeast 37th Avenue
Portland, Oregon. 97211
Email: mercuryflatsgazette@gmail.com

Standard Address Number: 992-3705

Cover Photo: (Edited)
Mr. Michael Hlebechuk
San Miguel de Allende
Guanajuato, Mexico

Publishers Logo: Public Domain -
Generated by MS Co-Pilot 365 (Edited)

Editor: Rene Walsh
Atomic Mountain Press, L LC
Walnut Creek, California.

Font: 14-point Tahoma, for easy reading

DISCLAIMER:
No Artificial Intelligence (AI) was used in the creation of text within this work whatsoever.

DEDICATION:

Mr. Michael Hlebechuk

One of the few *really* smart people I've ever met in my life!

"Writing and reading decrease our sense of isolation. They deepen and widen and expand our sense of life: they feed the soul."

Anne Lamott

CONTENTS

PART I:
PERSONAL ESSAYS

THE NEGRO

Recently I came across an entry for the word "Negro" in the *1798 Encyclopedia Britannica*, the first American edition of the English project modeled upon the great *Encyclopedie*. This is the opening three paragraphs for the entry:

"NEGRO, *Homo pelli nigra*, a name given to a variety of the human species, who are entirely black, and are found in the Torrid zone, especially in that part of Africa which lies within the tropics.

"In the complexion of Negro's we meet with various shades; but they likewise differ far from other men in all the features of their face. Round cheeks, high cheekbones, a forehead somewhat elevated, a short, broad, flat nose, thick lips, small ears, ugliness, and irregularity of shape, characterize their external appearance. The Negro women have the loins greatly depressed, and very large buttocks, which give the back the shape of a saddle.

"Vices the most notorious seem to be the portion of this unhappy race: idleness, treachery, revenge, cruelty, impudence, stealing, lying, profanity, debauchery, nastiness and intemperance, are said to have extinguished the principles of natural law, and to have silenced the reproofs of conscience, They are strangers to every sentiment of compassion, and are an awful example of the corruption of man when left to himself."

I shouldn't be surprised at this blatant, racist description of the black race portrayed by educated white people during the age of the so-called Enlightenment. After all, these same educated white people owned slaves.

This seems to be the great incongruity during the period of the founding of our country by a group of rich, gentleman farmers that were wise for their times.

Nevertheless, it makes me sad that our country's most wise were even capable of such nonsense. Thank goodness we now live in the 21st century where such nonsense has been relegated to the dust bin of history. Right? I can imagine the reader, rolling their eyes and laughing out loud at such a statement.

A personal example of this type of nonsense took place during the manned-moon landing in 1969. The pastor of our small church was a huge fan of the space program and didn't want to miss the live television broadcast which took place during the scheduled Sunday evening service.

Instead of having the regular worship service, he brought in his television and we all watched the moon landing as it happened.

The pastor did read an inspirational chapter from the Bible before the event , but I still think it was really a cover for his real agenda that night.

Anyway, the event was spectacular and I remember pastor Taylor glued to the television screen, and jumping up with both fists raised in the air and cheering, when Neil Armstrong took that first small step for mankind.

During the event I remember another teenager asking his father why there weren't any black astronauts. I also remember quite vividly my own father's horrifying answer: "They can't send black men into space because they're too emotional." The other boys father thought about this a moment and just shrugged his shoulders, while the pastor quickly changed the subject and gave my father a very stern look.

I nearly dropped to the floor with complete embarrassment and thinking to myself, where does the old man pick up such stuff. At the tender age of fourteen I knew my father was full of stinking bull crap on this one. Later that week I tried to him he was dead wrong about why there were no black astronauts.

I told him his theory was illogical and the reason we didn't have black astronauts was due to educational and employment discrimination. "You and your logic," hollered my father. He then went on to say: "I work around these people every day." As if that gave credence to his pet theories on black people.

There was a hidden agenda with my father which greatly influenced his many colorful theories about blacks in general. He worked for the California Department of Transportation for many years. He was passed over numerous times for promotions that went to black men who he thought were unqualified.

That being said, my father was very good friends with

Oscar, a black man who he closely worked with on the road crew. My father and Oscar were similar in that they never finished high school, but got their G.E.D.'s later on after military service. Oscar had three boys and my father and me would go fishing with them on a regular basis. I remember it being one of the most joyful times in my life.

And then during the summer of 1968 we never went fishing again with Oscar and his boys. I remember that summer my father going on and on about how black people were great workers, but when they got together in a group they caused nothing but trouble. This was also the summer that Martin Luther King was assassinated and having to listen to my father sound off with righteous authority: "King set the black man back fifty years."

Part of the reason my father held so many nonsensical theories about black people was two-fold. Firstly, he was born and raised in a small conservative, all white county in Pennsylvania.

Secondly, his lack of a solid, formal education. He dropped out of the 8th grade but managed to get his G.E.D. after the Army, while working at an air conditioning job. He wasn't much of a reader. He only read technical manuals for work when trying to pass various exams.

My fathers knowledge base of history, literature, philosophy, and science was pretty much empty. When he did get excited about reading a book (which was rare), it was always about a current fad, the life story of a self-made Christian businessman or a particular conspiracy theory. Otherwise his primary reading was from the Bible. And it was mostly due to my father's example that I decided very early on in life to become a voracious reader of many subjects, including the autobiography of Malcolm X in high school.

Careful and clear thinking requires a certain rigor; it is a skill and like all skills, requires training, practice and vigilance. Something my father didn't have time for because he often worked two jobs. If only he had gone to night school and took a few courses in critical thinking or picked up a book with solid information once in a while, his life would have been much different.

My father spurned logic in favor of nonsense about black people because he tended to believe what he wanted to believe; tended to project his own biases or experiences upon situations; tended to generalize from a specific event; tended to let his feelings overcome a sense of objectivity; he was not a good listener; tended to oversimplify; often simply didn't know what he was talking about, especially in matters of general discussion.

My father rarely thought carefully about black people before he opened his mouth, but always allowed his feelings to get the better of him. Kind of like the rest of us at times.

The above observation about my father may seem a bit harsh. It is not meant to be. I loved my old man and there were many happy times growing up. This observation merely suggests that it is a natural human tendency to be subjective rather than objective, and that the untrained mind will usually take the path of least resistance.

This path is rarely through reason, which brings me to the difficulties that President Barack Obama has had to go through, not only these past five years but during his campaign for the White House. When reading about or listening to the kind of ignorant, conspiratorial garbage concerning our President, it occurs to me that we as a people haven't moved much beyond the outdated and stereotypical image of black people that was presented 213 years ago. How tragic for all of us.

GRAVE CONCERNS

[This essay was originally published for an upper division writing course in 1999. Later it was part of the essay collection of my now out-of-print book, *Raw Beginnings*.]

I first discovered cemeteries at the age of thirteen. This began a life-long passionate hobby of exploration and research into the rich history and the lives of those underneath the ground.

From that first cemetery experience I started a spiral, three-ringed notebook that I titled, "Grave Concerns." I logged important grave marker data into this notebook, as well as sketches and rubbings.

On that first day of discovery in January 1968 in a town called Hayward, California, I was walking the one-and-half miles to Bret Hart junior high, as I did hundreds of mornings before. But on that day it turned out to be unlike any other January day. The sky was a solid steel gray. Every now and then the sky would let loose with a torrent of ice pellets.

What was left of the brown, crunchy autumn leaves were being scattered about by a chilly wind that cut deep to the bone. On this day I was running late for school. I decided to take a shortcut through what we kids called the Plunge Park cemetery that lay directly behind the school.

Calling it an old cemetery would be a gross understatement. The crumbling markers, overgrown foliage and two big partially toppled trees clearly showed that no one really cared anymore.

I managed to crawl safely through a break in the dilapidated fence and attempted to quickly pass to the other side. My attempt failed. I would end up completely missing my first period class.

This was my first time in the place and

it made me feel quite uneasy, not because of the dead people, but of being caught by park officials in a place surrounded by no trespassing signs.

I found the neglected and crumbling grave markers with exotic symbols and inscriptions, fuel for my over-active imagination and passion for local history. It was in this day that my true education began in earnest.

What I learned from the many visits to this cemetery, and side visits to the local library, eclipsed anything I was taught in school at the time. This alternative educational process would have dramatic and life-changing effect on me as an adult.

As I walked among the various markers I noticed that the cemetery was neatly divided up into sections based on religion, ethnicity and trade. The smallest and most neglected section was Jewish. The Star of David still showed prominently but the names & dates unreadable.

The other smaller section was a mixture of Freemasons, Rosicrucian and Catholic. This section had the only three above ground crypts. All three were in a state of disrepair and had been vandalized over the years.

The biggest and most colorful section had been reserved for the "Woodsmen of the World." The names and dates were still readable with few exceptions. The dates went back to the 20's and 30's. These markers were not your typical, everyday rectangular stones lying flat or standing upright, but mostly granite shaped into the form of a tree trunk about four feet high.

I didn't find out until months later at the library what this "Woodsman of the World" inscription meant. This is when I started my notebook, so that I could keep all this newfound knowledge organized in my head. "Woodsman of the World" was a common inscription put on markers of those who were called "Wobbly" – a nickname given to workers who were members of the Industrial Workers of the World trade unionist movement.

The Wobblies were started in Chicago in June of 1905 by Big Bill Haywood of the Western Federation of Miners, and others who were dissatisfied with the lack of progress of the little old craft unions under Sam Gompers' American Federation of Labor. They were a defiant radical group of mostly Anarcho-Syndicalists, and they argued bitterly with socialists as to the value of trying to elect working-class congressmen. Their idea was to ultimately sign up all the workers in "one big union," improve their conditions, and eventually call a general strike to decide who was going to run the world – the workers or the bosses.

It was at one of these "woodsmen of the World" makers that I had an experience that cracked wide open my little provincial world of dead people and history. In the Spring of 1969, as I walked through the cemetery, I noticed a classmate sitting cross-legged against a

Wobbly marker. As I got closer he was just staring straight ahead, glassy-eyed. A thin syringe was inserted into his left index finger, just under the skin.

After pausing, I quickly moved on, my heart racing and butterflies dancing in my stomach. Later that day other classmates educated me about "skin-popping" heroin. The sight of my classmate that day was so disturbing that I buried myself even deeper into my world of books and arcane knowledge. The classmate I encountered that day in the cemetery died two years later from a drug overdose.

The summer following my awakening to the real world of heroin abuse, I spent inside the library researching everything I could find out about the Wobblies and other related topics. I eventually discovered Marxism. One day at the library I took down a huge condensed version of *Das Kapital* by Karl Marx, and attempted to read it. This was quite an undertaking for a 14-year old boy.

I managed, however, to read the inside book jacket and most of the introduction. Most of what was being said went way over my head but the passages about the working-class revolution fired up my imagination.

The other area of the Plunge Park cemetery that became prominent in my notebook as well as my heart was the Freemason section. The names and dates were often worn off the stones but the Masonic symbols and inscriptions stood the test of time. Symbols such as the pyramid with the all-seeing eye, the letter G, and the compass intrigued me enough to start a search in the library.

One of the local librarians claimed to be a Freemason and gave me some useful information and books to read. He even invited me to the local Scottish Rite of Freemasonry church, but I never felt comfortable taking him up on the offer. There was something weird about this guy and my gut told me to stay far and clear of him.

(Later I found out that he liked "cruising for young boys.") he did tell me that Freemasonry was one of the oldest and largest fraternal orders in the world.

The heritage of modern Freemasonry is derived from the organized guilds or unions of stonemasons, who constructed the beautiful cathedrals and other stately structures throughout Europe during the Middle Ages.

The skills and architectural genius of these craftsmen and their commitment to the highest standards of moral and ethical values, were universally applauded, and unlike other classes of people, were allowed to travel "freely" from country to country.

Thus, during this period, the word "free" was prefixed to the word mason, and these craftsmen, and generations of masons who followed, were referred to as Freemasons.

In 1971, about the time I was filling up my notebook with Freemasonry data, another dramatic and disturbing experience happened to me that shattered my small, bookish world forever. My mother was diagnosed with breast cancer and had to undergo a radical mastectomy. This hung over my world like an angry black cloud for quite a long time.

This experience petrified me to the core of my being, because I saw some outside force, which I had no control over, trying to take my mother away. The exotic and seemingly important knowledge that filled my notebook lay impotent before this force. I found myself spending more time in the Plunge Park cemetery. I would sit by one of my favorite grave markers and look up into the sky and just think.

I would think about the people buried there and what kind of lives they lived, and what tragedies they endured. I also tried to imagine life without my mother. It was impossible!

On more than one occasion the tears would flow down my face. During this intense time of my life the Plunge Park cemetery became the one place that was eternal, that did not change, that always remained stable like a rock.

It has been too many years since that first day I discovered the Plunge Park cemetery. Even now as I write this I have the urge to revisit that place of my boyhood with its many mysteries and crumbling history, and once again walk those same steps. But of course, now the view would be profoundly different, almost tragically different I fear.

The memory I have of this place and the spiral, three-ringed notebook that documents this memory, will always have a place in my heart as a monument to my boyhood, my alternative education, my classmate's death, my mother's near-death experience, that catapulted me upon a lifetime journey of finding the Truth.

POETRY AS SPIRITUAL PRACTICE

[This essay was originally published on a now defunct blog in 1995, and later included in the now out-of-print book, *Raw Beginnings*]

When I was a youth I always had a copy of Walt Whitman's *Leaves of Grass* in my backpack. In the chaotic and ever-changing world of 1970, it was standard issue for those of my generation who looked upon themselves as the modern-day equivalent of the Transcendentalist. I took it one step further and proclaimed it my "holy book."

Whitman's longest poem in this volume, "Song of Myself," is at once a proclamation of spirituality, individualism and freedom. He composed his poetry not as a way to make a living, but that of personal spiritual practice. And essentially that is how I have always approached my own reading and writing of poetry – a personal spiritual practice.

Poetry as spiritual practice comes in two parts. Firstly, is reading the poems of our civilization, plumbing the depths of abstraction to discovering great truths about the world we live in. Secondly, is writing your own poems, and making them part of your daily rituals, aspirations, and intentions.

And then by assuming certain attitudes and postures, contemplating and reciting poems, chants, hymns, prayers, mantras, songs, and scriptures, you make yourself an open and willing receptacle for life itself. In 1982, after having what some refer to as an "ah ha" moment, I composed the following poem:

THE DRIFTER

The drifter travels an empty highway
Frantically seeking his next birthday.
Finding not the answer but yet another
dream
He stumbles forward through history with
a scream.
Where will he find his mystical fate?

Does he know the hour is late?
When will he finally face his doom?
When will the wildflowers finally not
bloom?
Why does he choose this lonely path?
Does he know it may incur God's wrath?
Who is this being with his own story?
Could he be a footnote in history?
The drifter walks to a frantic inward beat
And the mystic drum never skips a beat.

It was during this time of my life that I was actively pursuing the study of the interior life via a New Age group. I was contemplating with a single-minded perseverance, at the same time absorbing the poetry of Rumi, Wordsworth, Blake, Tennyson, Milton, and Dante. When I combined this activity with long periods of juice fasting it had the same effect as LSD. The one lesson I took away from this was that life was a balancing act between interior wishes and ideals, and harsh outer reality.

For the next decade I pursued a course of poetry that attempted to reflect this new found balancing act between the inner and outer self. To the mystical poetry I was already reading, I added to my repertoire, T.S. Eliot, Ezra Pound, Robert Frost, Robinson Jeffers, and most of the beat poets. But I was still pretty much a True Believer. As the character, Fox Mulder, said on the television show, *The X-Files*: "I want to Believe!"

In 1994, I had just completed a two-year reevaluation of my entire life and belief system, and had another of one those "ah ha" moments. The following poem was the result:

MY RELIGION

I have found my own private religion;
A religion that has yet to be named
And hopefully never will.
It is an authentic religion.
Its creed my beating heart.
Its dogma my aging bones.
Its vision the synapses of my brain.
Its tradition my birth, childhood,
Adolescence, adulthood.

It is a living, breathing, vibrant religion.
I am its deity, savior, chief disciple,
Follower and critic all rolled in one.
It is an exclusive religion.
It is my religion.

This poem was also my way of telling the world that I rejected the rigid ideologies of the theist as well as the atheist. Both worldviews are based in a predetermined mythology: one being a panorama of gods, angels, demons, and an afterlife, the other being an intractable scientific materialism. I didn't want to be associated with either side. My compromise, if you will, was settling on a humanism with a small "h." This more agnostic view gave me the freedom to investigate the mysterious unknowns out there without submitting to blind faith.

Even though I declared myself a humanist I still use poetry as a personal spiritual practice. Now, this may seem a bit odd to some, but consider the misinformation about humanism and spirituality in general, and then you might understand my perspective. A perspective that is dead center between the two extremes. A perspective methinks a lot more people embrace than not.

I found this perspective explained quite admirably by Nicaraguan poet, Ernest Cardenal, in his epic masterpiece, *Cosmic Canticle*. The Cantiga's (or chapters) explore the mysteries of the Big Bang all the way through to the history of exploitation in the Americas. When I first read this epic volume in 2002 it had the same feel as when I first read Whitman's *Leaves of Grass*. I came full circle and was home once again.

THE ILIAD OF HOMER

[this essay was originally published on a now defunct blog in 2002. It went on to be included in the now out-of-print book, *Raw Beginnings*.]

The *Iliad* of Homer has been one of my favorite reads since I first discovered it in the 9th grade. Its epic expanse of war and human passion took me on a roller coaster ride of the imagination. The teacher that introduced me to this great piece of epic literature was so passionate about it that it seemed he was from another time and place.

When he read sections of the book to the class he became one of the participants in the story, and this passion washed over the class like a wave. Even the most non-committed student became interested in the outcome. This stated my love affair with Homer's *Iliad*.

Over the years my fondness for the *Iliad* became a protracted, serious hobby.

I even went so far as to read nearly one hundred books and articles about Homer and his time. At one point I even taught myself the most basic level of the Homeric dialect in order to read a few stanzas in the original. This was one of the most glorious highlights of my reading career.

I have read every translation of the *Iliad* that I could get my hands on. Powell's Bookstore in Portland, Oregon was an excellent resource, because at one point in my search it had at least nine different translations and scores of scholarly books. Powell's even had hardcover and paperback editions of the translations by Alexander Pope, who some experts think is the greatest translation of all time.

In 1976 I happened upon a copy of the Alexander Pope translation. It was the 1943 hardcover boxed Heritage First Edition, with illustrations by John Flaxman. On the inside cover it was autographed by heritage editor Carl Van Doren. Also enclosed was a letterhead from the Department of Classical Studies at U.C. Berkeley, authenticating the signature of Van Doren.This was indeed one of the greatest book finds of my entire life.

I was living in Napa, California at the time and was browsing through stuff at an estate sale. The book laying on a very nice antique table had a $75 price tag. The price was steep and I was unemployed, but I bought it anyway. It was enclosed in a protective plastic book cover and upon opening it the smell of history was intoxicating, and I held it to my face for several seconds before resealing it.

I have always been the type of person who puts more value on a good, quality, musty-smelling old book, than on trinkets, new clothes or a nice dinner out on the town with friends. My friend, Steffan at the time, upon reviewing my purchase said: "Why spend good money on this crap when you could have gotten a hooker in Frisco for the same money."

This was the striking difference between us but we were best friends anyway. He also commented that it was nothing more than expensive toilet paper for "some rich white ass." This seemed to be a theme with Steffan when it came to old books, or books that seemed "too thick and depressing." Nevertheless, he always cheerfully accompanied me on my book adventures to City Lights Books in San Francisco.

Regardless of my friends shocking commentary on books in general, I continued my love of old books and re-reading the *Iliad* about every five years religiously. Then on December 17, 2000, a disturbing event took this rare, old treasure away from me forever. On that day we had a house fire that forced us to live elsewhere for several months during the re-building.

Unfortunately, I had two boxes of old books, including my beloved *Iliad*, in the attic above the garage where the fire started. There was nothing left but ashes.

The loss of that book was devastating. I had already made plans to keep it well into my retirement and sell it for profit. Back in 1983 Powell's Books had looked at it and offered me $300.

The financial worth of this book was secondary. What truly disturbed me was the loss of a piece of history. I was in one sense an irresponsible curator of that piece of history. I have never forgiven myself for that mistake. Even after this my love and passion for the *Iliad*, that was sparked by a teacher so many years earlier, continues unabated.

THE HERETIC

[This essay was originally published on a now defunct blog in 2004. Later it became part of my collection in the now out-of-print book, *Raw Beginnings*.]

The literary form called the character novel, has had an immense impact on my intellectual life, ever since I first discovered at the tender age of fourteen, Willard Motley's prize winning novel, *Knock On Any Door*. This is the story of Nick Romano growing up in the Chicago slums. He was an alter boy at 12 and dead in the electric chair at 21.

The story of Nick Romano exposed me to a part of life that was unknown to me at the time. This composite story of a troubled street youth fired up my imagination and left me wanting to fread more of the same. I was fortunate enough to have had a sympathetic English teacher at the time, who recognized my passion for stories about people, and further exposed me to what he called "protest literature."

He gave me a short list to work from and at the top of that list was the novel, *Down These Mean Streets* by Pere Thomas. Also on the list was the play, *Westside Story*. From there I jumped into nonfiction literary treats such as *Blood in My Eye* by George Jackson. This literature of troubled youth had such a poignant impact on me that, I ended up with the unintentional result of working with these same kinds of troubled kids later in life.

From 1984 until 1988, I worked as an outreach worker and emergency services coordinator for Outside-In's street youth program. At the time, Outside-In was one of Portland, Oregon's premier socio-medical aid stations, which provided free counseling, referrals, emergency services, and a walk-in medical clinic for the down and out. It was here that I met many Nick Romano's with their own unique and passionate stories.

One lad I worked with went on to spend

five years in prison for arson, another committed suicide, while yet another died so young of HIV/AIDS. The lives and stories of these street kids eventually became too overwhelming and I had to leave that part of my life behind and move on to other things.

My fascination with troubled souls is still alive and well today. I have collected around twenty-five character novels which I consider keepers, to be read and re-read many times over. The characters in these novels are most often dubbed anti-heroes by the mainstream literary establishment, and often referred to in negative terms: lonely oddballs, self-absorbed individualists, mental cases, contrarians, nonconformists, deviants, as well as many other names too numerous to list here.

The better label for these self-destructive and colorful misfits would be **heretic**. Whether these character's heretical lifestyle and thinking are merely self-made protective barriers against normal society, or a way of accessing the ultimate truth about existence, they have one thing in common: they were born heretics, held hostage by their genetics, social culture, and family upbringing and had no choice but to be who they were.

The best of these character novels that truly represents the heretic is *Against Nature* by J.K. Huysmans. The copy I own is a translation (and one of the best) from the French by Robert Baldick. The book hit the literary scene of 1884 like a cosmic big bang. Oscar Wilde found this the "strangest book that he had ever read" and it became a key text for his own writings.

Emile Zola called the book "a terrible blow to Naturalism." The general public condemned it as a work of depravity. In colorful and flowery prose the book tells about the strange, exotic and perverse pleasures and practices of one Duc Jean Floresses des Esseintes, a composite character of several "gorgeous dandies of the time."

Some have accused Huysmans of writing about himself in the thinnest of disguises.

As Robert Baldick writes in his introduction: "Des Esseintes is more than his creator's alter ego and the quintessential Decadent. He is also, and above all else, the modern man par excellence, tortured by that vague longing for an elusive ideal which we used to call the *mal du siecle*; torn between desire and satiety, hope and disillusionment; painfully conscious that his pleasures are finite, his needs infinite."

As the character Des Esseintes was the epitome of the heretic during his time of the 1880's, so Nick Romano was the epitome of the heretic during his time ofb the 1950's. Both of these characters in their own uniquely tragic way captured Baldick's "the modern man par excellence." Both Romano and Des Esseintes were painfully aware that their pleasures were indeed "finite and their needs infinite."

And I have come to the conclusion that the street youth I worked with and cared so deeply about in the 1980's suffered the same depravity that cursed Des Esseintes. Heretics young or old, from all ages of history and well into the future, will always be who they are, and no matter how much we have sympathy for them, or even try to help protect them from themselves, they will continue to follow the path that fate has bestowed upon them.

THINGS THAT GO BUMP

[Originally published on a now defunct blog in 2007, and later in the book, *Raw Beginnings.*]

things that go bump in the night had not concerned me since my teenage years, when an overactive imagination ruled my world. But on October 18, 2005, I was forced to confront one of those bumps. My partner Ave and I were part of a Halloween group tour of the Portland Shanghai Tunnels, led by Michael jones, Curator of the Cascade Geographic Society.

For those of my readers who are unfamiliar with the "tunnels" underneath the city of Portland, a little bit of background history is a must. In the words of Michael Jones: "Shanghaiing was an illegal maritime practice where able-bodied men – sailors, loggers, cowboys, sheepherders, ranch hands, construction workers, and vagabonds, in addition to other hard workers who were either employed or who frequented the waterfront, were grabbed or kidnapped and sold to sea captains who forced them to work aboard their ships for no pay."

Mr. Jones continues: "Portland was unique because trap doors known as *deadfalls* were used to drop the unsuspecting victims into the Portland Underground, where they were forcibly held in cells until the ship was ready to set sail. From 1850 to 1941, the so-called Victorian-refined Portland was known as the Unheavenly City, creating an even greater opportunity for men to find themselves aboard a ship bound for the Orient."

Ave and I arrived a bit early at the designated meeting place: Hobo's Restaurant, located on Northeast 3rd avenue, in the heart of Old Chinatown. This area used to be called the Old North End and was one of the most violent and crime-ridden neighborhoods of Portland at one time.

While waiting the arrival of Michael Jones, Ave enjoyed some happy hour food while I had a glass of amber ale.

After Mr. Jones arrived we joined the rest of the tour group which numbered fifteen, outside the back door of the restaurant, in a little walled-in outside patio. After giving his introductory speech on the rules of behavior and safety tips, he made sure everyone was dressed properly. Jones then passed out small flashlights. He took us outside and around the corner to 4th avenue, where a heavy plywood door with a huge padlock, took us down a flight of decrepit stairs where the tour began.

The first leg of the tour brought us immediately into a large room with a dirt floor that can only be described as trashy, dusty, decrepit, musty, dirty, dank, hot, and suffocating with unbearably low ceilings. In fact, these same words can be consistently used to describe everywhere we went on the tour. We didn't traverse any of the actual tunnels, although we walked long dark corridors with rooms of differing sizes. The amount of trash was staggering, even though Mr. Jones and his volunteer crew had cleaned out much of the debris to make the tour safe.

Between the dirt, dust, rotten odors, and low ceilings, and the incredible hot air generated from the ceiling pipes from businesses on street level, made the tour a little bit unpleasant for my taste. Along the various passages, Mr. Jones would stop and relate historical trivia about the tunnels and some rather juicy tidbits about Portland in bygone days. Since it was a Halloween tour he threw into the mix tales of ghostly visitors and sounds.

Most of the stories were from volunteer crews who helped clean out the trash. Some stories came from individuals who were on past tours. Mr. Jones related one of these stories that was quite striking in its content. The first large room we entered, Mr. Jones showed us the remnants of an oven where the bodies of kidnapped men were cremated, because they had died in the "cells" awaiting transfer aboard a ship.

Mr. Jones told the group that a man from one of his tours caught on video recorder a disembodied head floating about the room. I don't remember the reason why this video is no longer available, but as Jones related this ghostly tale, I noticed my partner, Ave with that famous smirk on her face, and I thought to myself: yeah right! Just another bullshit story. I had to admit however, this story at the beginning of the tour set the appropriate mood of overpowering dread and excitement.

What added to this infectious excitement and anticipation of the unknown was the attitude and physical appearance of Mr. Jones. Michael Jones is indeed a first-class spinner of tall tales and his remarkable knowledge of Portland's past gives him an immediate air of credibility. His rotund body, full beard, long hair and incredible squinty eyes, makes him the perfect tour guide for something like this.

During the rest of the tour Mr. Jones showed us some of the remarkable finds of his volunteer crews. We saw eating implements, belt buckles, shoes, clothing, plates, a silver cigar box, jewelry, small holding cells, and other intriguing tidbits from the late 19th century Portland.

One of the interesting things we were shown was an actual trapdoor (*deadfall*) underneath where the old Erickson's Saloon was located. The various holding cells were miserable cramped, hot and dirty. It's a wonder that anyone survived down there long enough to make it aboard a ship.

The tour ended an hour and a half later in a room just before we excited to street level in front of Hobo's. During the last ten minutes, something strange happened to me. The incident took place in the last room where the group had assembled in a semi-circle around Mr. Jones to hear his closing speech. I stayed towards the back of the group because I was feeling claustrophobic. The oppressive atmosphere made me want to get outside as soon as possible.

As Mr. Jones talked I was just observing the backs of the crowd, including the back of my partner Ave. Then it happened! I felt a strong, deliberate and slow stroke from the spot between my shoulder blades down my spine just above my butt. It felt just like someone's open palm. I heard the faint sound of something sliding on my jacket material.

I immediately thought someone in the group was playing a prank on me. I stood my ground without moving for a few seconds and then quickly whirled about.

Nobody was there. Just a foot of dusty space and the cement wall. To my immediate right was the other wall a foot away. To my left, about ten feet away were two members of the tour looking straight ahead, absorbed in what Mr. Jones was saying. No one else was near me.

If one of those two people did play a prank they would have had to be extremely fast and deadly quiet. There was enough debris on the dirt floor to make any movement very noticeable. My peripheral vision would have had to be completely on the fritz also. They just seemed too far away. As we all excited to the street I quickly walked by the two men and up the wooden stairwell. As I emerged. Mr. Jones asked if that was everybody. I said there are still two guys down there. He quickly did a head count and all fifteen of us were on the street. He went back down and looked around – nobody was there.

I am not a believer in ghosts! In fact,

I consider myself a hard boiled skeptic. What happened that evening I can't explain. Could it have been the result of the glass of beer before the tour, the anticipation and excitement generated by Mr. Jones, or my famous overactive imagination on the re-bound?

I guess it will just be one of those mysterious, unexplained events that I'll never be able to resolve one way or the other.

A WALK ON THE BEACH

[Composed in December 2003 for an advanced creative writing class but never published until now.]

The sky was mostly one big sheet of solid whit clouds. Off in the distance, over the water, there were large gaps of blue starting to form over the horizon. The gentle, but not too cold, breezy wind was welcomed on this January day at the Oregon coast.

My dog Murphy and me decided to take a long early morning walk on the beach and explore. We had no plan, no goal and no expectations other than what nature had in store for us. We walked for over an hour. I enjoyed the coming and going of the waves, while Murphy ran along sniffing and exploring every little nook and cranny. At one point we got too near the water and a sneaker wave caught us by surprise getting our feet wet.

We sat down to rest in the sand against a big log. Murphy sat next to me peering out at the waves with her ears up, like she was waiting for something to happen. I followed her gaze and looked deeply into the ocean but couldn't even see an oil tanker on the horizon. She finally calmed down and laid her head in my lap. I continued staring at the water and thinking about the eternal coming and going of the waves – producing a hypnotic effect on me.

This coming and going of the waves reminded me about the ever-changing aspect of life. I was never immune to sudden life changes and often it took me months or years to integrate change in my life. As I sat there thinking, I was suddenly assaulted by a tragic memory that happened two years before.

Once again I found myself in the middle of our small kitchen. Black smoke was pouring in from the garage, engulfing the whole house. I was screaming at the top of my lungs,

calling the names of my three dogs,
thinking they were still inside the garage.
As my eyes became swollen by the
smoke, panic dug its talons into me. I
could hardly catch my breath and when I
did it was an oppressive, hot pain.
Blackness enveloped me!

When I looked down at my feet I saw a
thin layer of murky twilight. I had to get
out quickly, so I started walking out of
the kitchen. I hit something hard and it
brought me to my knees in a coughing fit.
I crawled forward following the murky
twilight and hit a chair. I had to get out
now because it was becoming impossible
to breath.

I stood up with the idea of running to the
front door but everything was black. I ran
towards what I thought a safe path and
crashed into something big and hard. I
was on my knees again. I was so
disoriented I didn't know what room I
was in. I stood up again and walked
forward only to hit something soft.

It was a neighbor. He grabbed my arm tightly and led me to the front porch where others were starting to gather to help.

Suddenly, Murphy licking my hand broke my reverie. I was back on the beach watching the coming and going of the waves. I looked at my watch and nearly an hour had passed. We got up and started walking back to the beach house. The assaultive memory still lingered and I thought long and hard why I became so panicked during our house fire.

Panic was not my typical response to a crisis. For many years I had volunteered and worked for Metro Crisis Service and Outside-In, respectively. I was always given praise for having a cool head during the most serious crisis. While transporting a battered woman to a women's shelter, myself and another Metro volunteer were pursued by her husband and five of his biker friends for a dozen blocks, before a police car intervened.

Another situation happened while working at Outside-In. A female street youth came into our daytime drop-in center in a panic claiming someone was going to kill her. Moments later another female youth bolted through the front door wielding a butcher knife making threats.

I stood in front of the first youth, shielding her from the attacker. I spent the next three minutes talking down the assailant. The police arrived quickly and the attacker fled but was captured and arrested several blocks away. As before, I got through the situation with calm and no injury to myself or others.

At Metro Crisis and Outside-In, I was a dispassionate outside observer during times of crisis. Whether pursued by angry bikers or confronted by violent street youth, there has always been a window of hope and opportunity for rationale dialogue. But during the house fire I was the one being victimized and my animals and partner were put at great risk. Being surrounded by smoke and flames gives you no opportunity to interact with your attacker. Fire has no face, no emotion, and no brain to make a connection with and offer reason. It just burns and consumes relentlessly and destructively.

The sheer panic of not even having the hope of controlling such an attacker is horrifying, and no amount of preparation or training can overcome that. My deep thoughts about this issue came to a screeching halt as I fell head over heels over a small tangle of green algae on the beach. Murphy thought I was playing and stood over we wagging her tail.

We finally arrived back at the beach house and Murphy had a big drink of water and then retired to a cushion near the fireplace. I made myself a cup of tea and grabbed my notebook to write down the details of our walk.

As I opened the yellow notebook, a memory from many years ago settled upon me. This notebook reminded me of the first notebook I started keeping as a youth. That first notebook was about my visits to a local cemetery and sketching, rubbings and other information I gleaned from those visits. I had managed to save this special notebook for many years afterward until that fateful day of the house fire. It burned up with lots of other irreplaceable writings, pictures, documents and mementos.

I quickly pushed that memory aside and diligently wrote down the details of my morning walk with Murphy. After my journal entry, I grabbed another cup of tea and sat in an over stuffed chair before the massive picture window looking out towards the ocean. Off in the distance I barely discerned the vague image of a ship on the horizon, probably an oil tanker. As I watched this ghostly image fade into nothingness, my thoughts once again returned to the house fire.

I was sitting on the curb opposite my house, holding my sister-in-laws dog, Clair, who had been staying with us a few days. A drizzling rain had a sedative and muted effect on the cacophony that surrounded me. Several neighbors stood behind me, one even offered me a glass of red wine. People from surrounding streets were converging on the wild scene. Where I was sitting offered me a perfect view of the house between two parked fire engines.

Black smoke billowed out of the opened front door, while white streamers of smoke seeped out of every orifice of the structure. Amid all this noise and strife a strange sound hit my ears. The firemen on the roof succeeded in cutting a vent hole nearest the garage. A small pillar of fire blew through the vent hole momentarily as the firemen pumped gallons of white foam into the attic.

As the black smoke started turning white another team of firemen rushed into the open front door. It would be an hour and a half before the all clear signal was given.

As I continued sitting on the curb, now very damp from the drizzling rain and shaking slightly from the cold, a well-meaning person put their hand on my shoulder and asked if I was all right. I wanted to blurt out, "Of course I'm not all right. My fucking house is burning down!" Instead, I just sat there, thinking about the six boxes in the attic of a lifetime of memorabilia that had already been reduced to ash.

At that moment the strangest recollection came to me. Thirty years previously, I had read the biography of Aldous Huxley. In that book it is mentioned how Huxley reacted to his Los Angeles mansion burning to the ground during a severe grass fire.

A reporter asked him how he felt knowing that a lifetime of manuscripts, mementos and pictures were being consumed by flames. Huxley reportedly grinned real big and said, "I feel very clean now." Sitting on the curb watching my own past go up in flames brought tears.

Like Huxley before me I was being given a chance to put the past behind me and start fresh. But unlike Huxley, I had no clever phrases to dazzle those standing around me.

My cup of tea had grown cold as I sat before the big picture window deep in thought. The sky was much cloudier now and the wind had picked up considerably. Almost two hours had gone by. The memory of the house fire was different this time.

It seemed like a thousand years in the past, and the usual mental hand wringing I had engaged in over the past two years now seemed quite trivial. All this time I was attempting to hold on to the past and in some ways it kept me from doing the business at hand in the present.

I got up from the chair, stretched, looking over at Murphy. It was time for another walk.

ON THE DEATH OF A BELOVED CAT

[This essay was first published on a now defunct blog in December 2010. It has been out-of-print until now.]

Dexter lived on Earth nineteen years. My partner, Ave Marie, found her in a Safeway grocery parking lot in another neighborhood while grocery shopping. Attempts to find who the kitten belonged to utterly failed. She was a beautiful calico cat with one of the most sweetest dispositions you want in a cat.

Dexter was a timid kitty with a fragile personality. She was easily spoofed by the most common interactions that are typical of a cats life. Whether it was a crazed, kamikaze bumble bee, a curious hummingbird, or loud noise from the street, she would react as if it was the end of the world.

During her senior years it was the simple things that mattered to her.

During the nice weather she would lay under our fig tree or curl up in one of our planter boxes. She would lay there for hours watching life about her. The few things that would disturb her naps was an errant butterfly, a busy bee, or the swoosh of a curious hummingbird.

During the bad weather she still wanted to hang outside. We built her a small kitty house against the side of the house with a warm blanket and bowl of water. She would hunker down and watch the wind and rain come and go. If the weather really got bad she would come inside.

Another pleasure of Dexter's was vanilla bean ice cream. For the last five years she enjoyed a teaspoon of ice cream several times weekly. It got to be such a habit that if we forgot, she would position herself on the table behind the couch, wait and stare at us.

It wasn't until the last several years of her life that she truly became affectionate.

Before that she seemed fine being an observer on the periphery of our family. And she didn't mind staying outdoors as much as she could. The last year and a half, however, she voluntarily came inside to visit and snuggle with us.

During her life she had to put up with four other cats and three dogs who she managed to tolerate at a distance. If the others got too crazy she would flee the room and retire to a warm niche in the third bedroom we used as an office. There she would snooze and dream uninterrupted.

It was six months ago that Dexter started losing weight and looking quite wispy and bony. The vet suggested giving her some heavy cream or ice cream every night. Sometimes my partner, Ave, had to get a wet warm cloth and give her a bath, because Dexter wasn't taking care of herself. Because of her teeth she got wet food most of the time.

During the last month of her life

Dexter lost more weight and got bonier. We tried everything to keep her bulked up but nothing seemed to work. At this point she was almost living off cream. We knew she wouldn't be around this holiday season. We crossed our fingers and said a prayer. We spent much more time with her, making a big fuss and always talking to her.

The day before her death started out quite wet and foggy but by mid-afternoon the sky was mostly clear with a temperature of 58-degrees. She lost all desire to eat anything. We got a baby dropper and would make sure she got a squirt of milk and several of water. She looked like skin pulled over a bag of bones.

I let her outside under the fig tree while closely monitoring her so she could enjoy the day. She spent the afternoon moving about the yard, following the sun rays. I brought her in around 4:30 pm and gave her lots of pets and hugs. She purred a lot and stared at me intensely with those big, beautiful brown eyes. She retired to the bedroom and took a very long nap on one of the dog beds.

Ave and both agreed that Dexter probably wouldn't make it through the night. Ave brought her to bed at 11:30 pm and put her between us. Dexter stayed which was unusual because she never slept with us in all of her 19 years. At 1:30 am Dexter started moving about so I took her to the front room and put her in her kitty bed.

On Dexter's final day of life I got up at 7:30 am. I found her sleeping underneath the couch curled up next to the heat vent. She was alive but awfully weak. I was glad it was my day off so I could be with her. Ave left for work and I decided to go have coffee at the cafe and read the newspaper. Before leaving, I gave Dexter a big kiss.

I came back home at 9:30 am and Dexter was still alive but so weak she couldn't stand on her own.

Ave called around 11:30 am for an update. I moved her to her favorite red blanket near the window so she could see outside. I sat with her and read a book and took breaks to talk to her and what a good girl she was. It turned into a beautiful fall day, breezy, clear skies, 70-degrees, and colorful leaves bursting out everywhere. It was the kind of day Dexter would have enjoyed under different circumstances.

By 3:00 pm Dexter appeared unresponsive. She seemed in a coma. I did hear a slight purr when I petted her however. At 4:45 pm, I knew she would go anytime so I went outside and prepared her grave under the fig tree. Coming back in the house I noticed her body in a different position like she was stretching. Her mouth was open. I put my hand on her and nothing. I waited until 5:30 pm just to make sure but she was definitely gone. I sat there with her and cried a bit and remembered some of the good times we had these past 19 years.

PART II:
OTHER SUCH STUFF

A CONVERSATION BETWEEN GENERATIONS

I

The blistering sun hung low in the sky over the small town of Lucerne Valley among the shimmering sands of the Mojave Desert.

I sat on the front porch of the Lucerne Valley market with an ice cold orange soda pop. As I paused chugging my soda, out of nowhere, a Chemehuevi Elder walked up to me. His eyes held the wisdom of many seasons.

II

We talked together about things in general: the weather, orange soda pop, and life in general.

Reflecting on the years that had passed, I turned to the Elder saying,

"I sometimes wonder what comes after

all this. Death is a mystery to me. I've spent a lifetime contemplating it," as I gestured to the horizon.

The Elder nodded, his voice calm and steady.

"In our tradition, death is not an ending but a passage. The spirit continues its journey, moving beyond the physical world. We believe the ancestors watch over us, guiding each new soul to a place of peace."

III

I listened, comforted by the thought.

"I've always hoped there's something more. Something beyond pain, regret, and longing."

The Elder smiled gently.

"What matters is how we live, how we honor the earth, and those who walked before us.

The afterlife is shaped by the kindness and respect we show in this one."

IV

As the light faded, the Elder and me got up and moved to the parking lot of the market. The conversation lingered, echoing across the desert – two lives, bridging worlds, sharing stories about death and what lies beyond. In the quiet of the Mojave, I felt a sense of peace settle within me, carried on the wind of ancient wisdom.

ON THE PROBLEM OF EVIL:
A Dialogue Between Two Friends

ABSTRACT:

Two old men who have been best friends for the past 40 years meet once a week at the Rose & Thistle, a local tavern in Northeast Portland, to play chess and discuss life in general and the problems of the world.

CHARACTERS:

Angus – a retired professor of religion from Reed College. Age 72. Was a staunch Presbyterian but left the church to study Sufism. Leans liberal on most issues.

Nick – a retired Detective Captain from the Portland police Bureau. Age 68. Italian extraction. Considers himself a good Catholic and leans conservative on most issues.

NICK: [*Tackling his second pint, starts musing about the civilian death toll in the on-going conflicts in Ukraine, Iran and Palestine*] How could a loving God allow such evil to exist?

ANGUS: That is indeed complicated. However, instead of trying to justify the ways of God to man, maybe we should think more of justifying man's ways to God.

NICK: That would take forever!

ANGUS: An eternity, I suppose.

NICK: And so evil people like Putin, the Mullahs and Netanyahu will still be forgiven in the end?

ANGUS: Possible. I've been reading a text from the early Middle Ages, the *Vision of Saint Paul*, which is an account of the apostle's journey into the underworld. There he meets a man engulfed in the fires of purgatory. But the man is not in pain.

Instead, he is smiling. Why? Because he knows that three thousand years later one of his descendants will become a priest and, at his first Mass, that same priest will pray for him and release him from his suffering. Saint Paul realizes that three thousand years in purgatory is nothing compared with eternity. The sinner has taught him the meaning of patience.

NICK: I'm not sure I'd be prepared to spend three thousand years in pain. It would be simpler not to sin in the first place.

ANGUS: That is rather the idea.

[*Angus moved his chess piece and said "check." He then took a swallow of beer.*]

NICK: God must be a miserable old bugger, really, when you think of the wickedness human beings get up to; all that sin.

ANGUS: That may be true. If God is aware of the human condition then how can he be content? But perhaps we have to think about the divine presence in a different way; not as what he is, but what he is not. In other words, not human, and not liable to emotion. The concept of happiness perhaps has no subject. It exists outside ourselves, unrelated to any specific human being.

NICK: Then why do we all want to have it?

ANGUS: Because we are human.

NICK: And therefore we suffer.

ANGUS: Yes, Nick.

NICK: So what you are saying is that God does not know happiness; even though he is supposed to be omniscient? I don't understand how that works.

ANGUS: John Stuart Mill argued that happiness is not something that can be achieved by striving for it. You have to pursue some other goal and...

NICK: So happiness is an accident?

ANGUS: Possibly. Schopenhauer defined it as the temporary absence of pain.

NICK: And that is the best we can hope for?

ANGUS: Perhaps, but not necessarily.

NICK: Oh, Angus, this is all too deep for me.

ANGUS: Me too. Life still has many pleasures; not least the company of our delightful wives. Let us enjoy that while we may.

[*The two men finish their second pints and continue in silence finishing the chess game. Angus makes a quick move and exclaims – "checkmate." Then gives Nick a big smile.*]

NICK: Okay, once again you win. I definitely need to brush up on some good strategies for next week. Now let's leave the idea of happiness alone and pursue one last point. What is true contrition? Could a man be too contrite, making a confession that was so out of proportion to the crime that it becomes a form of attention-seeking? I'm thinking of Putin, the Mullahs and Bibi, here.

ANGUS: Sometimes the admission of sin could almost be a kind of vanity.

NICK: Really!!!

ANGUS: I want to say something about proportional penitence. Any request for forgiveness is not the property of the perpetrator alone. It must be freely given and freely received.

[*Nick grabs a handful of mixed nuts, eats them loudly and swallows the last mouthful of beer in his pint glass.*]

NICK: Go on. I'm interested…

ANGUS: The confession and the appeal must allow room for the victim – if he or she were still alive – to forgive with a whole heart. See, Nick, there has to be a mutual understanding of what has taken place. A time for recognition and a place for silence: forgiveness may be absolute but it cannot be taken for granted. It must be re-acknowledged each time we sin. But this is vital. Without forgiveness, we are condemned to the past. Forgiveness gives us a path to our future.

NICK: Ahhh, yes. I see it now clearly!

DEATH ROW DIALOGUE

SCENE: An 8X8 concrete cell. Dim light. A narrow bed bolted to the wall. Half eaten last meal lay on the bed. It's 10:00 pm. Two hours before execution time.

Kwame: Ghana born, early 40's, worn and hollowed out. A street pimp who brutally murdered one of his girls, chopped up her body and disposed of it in a landfill.

Robert: Late 50's, African-American, a prison chaplain, Iraq war veteran, calm but weathered.

[*The door buzzes. It opens. The door clanks shut. Robert gestures toward the empty stool.*]

ROBERT: Mind if I sit?

KWAME: Don't really matter. I guess you're paid to do this.

ROBERT: I'm here because I want to be. Not everyone wants company at a time like this. I thought you might.

[*Kwame stares at the floor*]

KWAME: I don't know what you want from me. I'm not like your other lost sheep. I've done things. Bad things. I ruined lives. I killed her. She trusted me. That was her biggest mistake. And I ended her life. How could any God forgive that?

ROBERT: Forgiveness isn't about what you deserve, Kwame. It's about the depth of mercy that's offered.

[*Kwame lets out a bitter laugh.*]

KWAME: I was a pimp. A dealer. A murderer. You're wasting your time.

ROBERT: You're not the monster others say you are. You're a man who made terrible choices. Christ forgave a thief while they were both dying on the cross.

KWAME: I want to believe that. I just don't know if I can. I feel empty inside. Like my soul left long ago.

ROBERT: That emptiness is grief. Let it open you – don't let it close you down. Can I ask you something? What do you think forgiveness is?

KWAME: Forgetting. Pretending it didn't happen. That's why it feels fake. Nothing I did can be undone.

ROBERT: You're right. Forgiveness doesn't erase the crime. You're here because justice matters in the big picture.

KWAME: Then what's the point? If I rot till I die, how does forgiveness change anything?

ROBERT: It changes YOU. Justice deals with the past. Forgiveness deals with what the past does to your soul.

KWAME: So guilt's optional now?

ROBERT: No. But despair is.

KWAME: Sorry preacher man, but you weren't there when she looked at me with those begging, desperate eyes. [*A flash of pain crosses Kwame's face.*] I see her every night. That's my sentence. That's my karma. I deserve it.

ROBERT: Deserving punishment and receiving God's mercy aren't opposites. [*Kwame looks up, making direct eye contact with Robert.*] Christ and the thief hung side by side on the cross.

KWAME: So what about her? Forgiveness feels like stealing peace at her expense.

ROBERT: It doesn't steal justice. It refuses to let evil have the final word.

KWAME: Then why do I feel like a fraud listening to you?

ROBERT: Because you think your sin is bigger than Christ's mercy.

[*Kwame gives a big scoff.*]

KWAME: So God just wipes the slate clean?

ROBERT: No. He calls you REDEEMED! Forgiveness is the door. Not the finish line.

[*Kwame's shoulder's slump.*]

KWAME: I still wake up a killer 24/7.

ROBERT: You wake up a man being remade.

KWAME: What if I can't forgive myself?

ROBERT: Then stop arguing with God. [*Kwame stiffens, sits upright.*] Self-forgiveness isn't a feeling. It's obedience.

KWAME: That feels wrong.

ROBERT: You're not the judge.

KWAME: I used people my whole life.

Now I want mercy. That makes me a hypocrite.

ROBERT: It makes you honest.

KWAME: If God forgives me [*Long pause.*] does that mean she has to also?

ROBERT: No. Forgiveness can't be forced on the victim.

KWAME: I don't know how to live with what I've done.

ROBERT: You won't learn tonight. But you can start living TOWARD God this moment, here now!

KWAME: You really think He still wants me after the horrible thing I did?

ROBERT: I think He's been waiting.

KWAME: Pray with me, preacher man. But don't pray easy words. [*Robert nods. Kwame bows his head, hands over his face.*]

ROBERT: God of mercy…You see every sin, every regret, every tear shed in this cell. He brings You nothing but truth. And asks for what he doesn't deserve. Teach him repentance without despair. Forgiveness without pride. Hope without illusion. Amen.

[*Kwame swallows hard, tears in his eyes.*]

KWAME: Amen

Silence. The BUZZER sounds faintly outside the cell.

FADE OUT.

ABOUT THE AUTHOR

Ben Douglass is a 71-year old Indie writer who has been residing in the Pacific Northwest for the past 44-years. He often refers to himself as a grumpy old white guy with Type 2 diabetes, survivor of prostate cancer, an attitude the size of the Grand canyon, and a sense of wonder as big as the Milky Way galaxy.

His cultural interests include Celtic folk music, the old English comedies on BBC America, foreign films (especially by Akira Kurosawa & Werner Herzog), and the theater. He reads numerous international magazines and journals on a regular basis.

His hobbies are few. For the past 55 years he has been an aficionado of Homeric literature. In his humble opinion, the Iliad & Odyssey are the greatest examples of heroic epic writing ever produced by humankind.

For the past 38-years he has lived

in the Concordia neighborhood of Northeast, Portland, Oregon, with his partner Ave Marie, four cats and one dog. When he's not spending time with them, he writes essays, plays, stories, and novels to amuse himself and others.

The authors books can be ordered at any bookshop in North America and most parts of Europe. For easy access, the reader can go to his book page and buy direct:

https://bendouglassbooks.com

Wholesalers can order direct with a 40% discount by emailing the publisher at:

mercuryflatsgazette@gmail.com

ABOUT THE EDITOR

Rene Walsh was born in 1952 in Chico, California. He attended San Jose State from 1970 until 1976, graduating with a Bachelor of Science in Electronics Technology and a Master of Science in Electronics Technology. He went on to work in the aerospace industry until 2006. After retirement he attended the University of San Francisco, graduating with a Masters of Fine Arts in creative writing in 2010.

Since then he has done extensive contract work as a technical writer and editor. Currently he is the owner/publisher of Atomic Mountain Press.

ABOUT
MERCURY FLATS PUBLISHING
[*an imprint of Atomic Mountain Press, LLC.*]

Dedicated to reprinting forgotten works by various misfits, outsiders, and rebels. Also, to highlight the works of new independent authors who want nothing to do with the big corporate publishers. The underlying concept here is based on a few simple propositions:

A) That to be a success under the current definition is highly toxic – wealth, fame and power are a poison cocktail;
B) That this era of triumphal capitalism glorifies the dreariest human traits like greed and self-interest as good and natural;
C) That the "winners" version of reality and history is deeply lame and soul-rotting stuff.

Given this, it follows that the truly interesting and meaningful lives and real adventures are only to be had on the margins of what Kenneth Rexroth called "the social lie."

It's with dropouts, misfits, dissidents, renegades and revolutionaries, against the grain, between the cracks and among the enemies of the state that the good stuff can be found.

Fortunately, there is a mighty subterranean river of testimony from the disaffected, a large cache of hidden history, of public secrets overlooked by the drab conventional wisdom the MERCURY FLATS PUBLISHING aims to tap into. A little something to set against the crushed hopes, mountains of corpses, and commodification of everything. We think, it's the best thing Western Civilization has going for itself.

Tahoma Font - Usage/Design/History/

This font and the 14-point size was deliberately used in this publication for "easy reading" and to help those disadvantaged folks with sight problems.

Tahoma is a humanist sans-serif typeface designed by Matthew carter for Microsoft in 1994, known for its legibility for sighted impaired people.

The name Tahoma is derived from the Native American name for Mount Rainier, a prominent feature in the Pacific Northwest region of the United States. This connection reflects the cultural significance and geographical context of the fonts design.

READERS NOTES

READERS NOTES